Copyright © 2022 by Sara Di Sorrenti

All rights reserved.

The Skonk of Tawk Valley © is a Registered Trademark. Sara Di Sorrenti has asserted her right under the Copyright, Designs and Patent Act 1998 to be identified as the author of this book.

This is a work of fiction. Names, characters, businesses, places, events and incidents are either the products of the author's imagination or used in a fictitious manner. Any resemblance to actual persons, living or dead, or actual events is purely coincidental.

No part of this book may be reproduced in any manner whatsoever without written permission except in the case of brief quotations embodied in critical articles and reviews. For permission requests, contact the author.

ISBN: 978-1-9192230-0-1
Published by Sara Di Sorrenti
First Printing, 2025

The Beginning

2ND EDITION

SARA DI SORRENTI

ILLUSTRATED BY KEEGAN BLAZEY

For Nancy My Mother

THE SUNRISES CAME AND THE SUNSETS GREW DIMMER

WITH WARM ACORN MILK

AND PORRIDGE WITH BERRIES

SKONK'S TUMMY WAS FULL

AND HE FELT MUCH MORE MERRY

SPRING ARRIVED WITH TALES TO TELL
PINK CASCADES OF BLOSSOM FEL

SOFTNESS OF A BREEZE DID PLAY
   AS PALED SUN LIT UP THE DAY

THE VALLEY MICE TO THE RESCUE CAME

TO PROTECT AND SAVE, AND THEIR FAME CLAIM

DEEP WINTER CAME
WITH LOTS OF SNOW

BUT BABY SKONK
       HE FELT NO COLD

WITH THE BURROW'S
        FIRE ALL AGLOW

HOW ON EARTH NOW CAN THIS BE
A ROUND BROWN BALL BENEATH THE TREE

THE SIGHS AND STARES OF PASSERS BY
WHO TOUCHED AND STROKED
AND JUST ASKED WHY...?

THE CURIOUS YOUNG SKONK
SOON FOUND HIS WAY OUTSIDE

TO ROLL IN SOFT GRASS
AND PLAY IN THE WILD

SPRING MEANDERED TO SUMMER AND SUMMER FELL INTO FALL

AS HE SPLASHED IN TAWK RIVER OH HE HAD SUCH A BALL!

THE BABY SKONK WAS CLEAND AND FED

AND LAID TO REST
           IN A NICE WARM BED

SOMEWHERE SAFE
           TO PLACE HIS HEAD

NORTHERN LIGHTS CAME TO DANCE
 SWIRLING COLOURS ALIVE TO PRAN

PINK PIGEONS FLEW BY

TO SAY HELLO!

BABY SKONK SO CHARMED BY THEIR ROSY GLOW

BABY SKONK LOVED HIS BATHTIME!

WITH SOAP FRAGRANT AND SOFT

SQUIRRELS HELPED TO BATHE HIM

SHOULDING HIS ARMS HIGH ALOFT

ICY STICKY CAKES

AND JELLY THAT WOBBLED

THESE TASTES OF DELIGHT

MADE BABY SKONK GOBBLE

BABY SKONK WOULD TO SLUMBER GO

TO DREAM AS SOFT AS A YEARLING DOE

THE END

www.ingramcontent.com/pod-product-compliance
Lightning Source LLC
Chambersburg PA
CBRC091504220426
43661CB00021B/1307